Win-Win-Win:

Collaborative Approach to Procurement in the Era of Digital Metamorphosis

Eric Dulin

Acknowledgements

As I mention in this book, procurement is tribal knowledge. I did not study procurement in my undergraduate or MBA program nor did I attend formal procurement training after joining my company. I learned procurement first by working in delivery and understanding what happens when contracts are structured poorly vs. properly. I then transitioned to sales and ultimately to procurement. I essentially learned from the people I worked for, the people I worked with, and the people who worked for me, not to mention from many stakeholders and suppliers that I have worked across 20+ companies, including HP, Accenture, Atos and DXC. That would be a book in itself, so I wanted to briefly mention a few of the many people who have influenced my strategy!

I have been very fortunate to have some amazing bosses throughout my career who gave me some artistic license to manage procurement teams and work through the challenges we faced. Special thanks to Phil Riley and Ryan Shadle. From a consulting and Procurement Outsourcing standpoint, they really helped me develop my strategy, and understand the processes and organizational structure to manage high-volume, fast-paced procurement operations. I also had some amazing client stakeholders over the years, and want to especially thank Steve Birks, John Todesco, and Chris Reynolds for allowing me to be part of their team!

I also thank Allen Yu and Sabina Rizvi for believing in my vision and giving me the opportunity to develop and implement an amazing process and team to support Digital growth and manage Procurement my way!

From the standpoint of who I worked with and who worked for me, I always tell my team they don't work for me, they work with me. There are too many people to thank, however, I do want to call out some of the amazing people that I worked with including Larry Fox, Anuradha Telikicherla, Ron Mansini, Ken White, Matthew Pippen, Andrew Davies, Jennifer Dominguez, Joel Salcedo, Pablo Landeros and Brittany Self. You were instrumental leaders in the teams that we managed! Your outstanding procurement and leadership abilities helped us successfully support our incredible stakeholders! Reunan Varene, Rash Sahota, Karen Alexander, Clotilde Solimeo, Keith Zylstra, Greg Walker, Diego Escorcia, Mona Yamartino and Erin Lee set the bar in supporting procurement clients and negotiating incredibly complex deals! Our collective experiences are what ultimately defined the Win-Win-Win strategy! We developed and implemented amazing teams, worked on complex and challenging negotiations, and delivered fantastic results as a team.

I also want to thank the incredible legal, security, data privacy and finance teams that worked hand-in-hand with the procurement team to execute our processes and successfully complete our negotiations. Procurement is not a stand-alone process and the tight collaboration with these critical teams makes it all happen! Special mention to Marc Shivers, Graham Edwards, Branda Glospie and Sefia El Yaakoubia for their support across many critical, complex and time constrained negotiations. You were fantastic!

To complete the circle, I have to thank some of the sales teams that I have worked with across multiple strategic supplier negotiations including Laura Rittmuller, Mitch Schneider, Kevin Stacy, Phil Wouden, and Jason Schaps. We learned to achieve the Win-Win-Win together!

I also want to thank my cousin Pat Dulin, owner of Dulin's Village Café in Vancouver WA, for reminding me of our family history, the challenges that we faced, and our never give up motto. I want to thank Professor Hitendra Chaturvedi who has been a mentor to me almost my entire life, and my son Eric Dulin who wrote three books before he graduated high school, for inspiring me to take the journey and write my own book.

Writing a book is harder than I thought! It's easy to come up with random thoughts but to articulate them in a relevant story is a challenge. I want to thank Shannon Constantine Logan for helping me tell the story, Terri Dilley for making the amazing cover, and Jessica Gang and Penny Dawson for editing and helping me publish this book.

Table of Contents

Introduction

In May 2020, I received an interesting email from Kelly, a recruiter for a global restaurant company asking if I was interested in applying for a Director of Technology Procurement position. This was an unusual time. First, I had just started a new job as the Chief Procurement Officer of Atos North America in January. Not only had I just started my new job, but I had also just finished establishing my procurement team, selling them on my procurement philosophy, and we were well on our way to implementing the previous strategies I had used with success at DXC Technology and Accenture.

Both the restaurant and the IT outsourcing industries were under immense pressure in the market. COVID pressured many industries to dramatically change their business models in response to changing customer requirements. Atos' clients were demanding immediate price cuts due to changes in their business models and suppliers, while sympathetic, were ultimately struggling to manage their own supply chain and customer challenges. From a restaurant industry standpoint, government mandated shutdowns in the US and abroad were having catastrophic impacts on the restaurant industry.

Did I really want to step back down to a Director role and manage a much smaller spend profile, during a time like this?

Ultimately, I accepted the position. The biggest deciding factor was that I knew the tremendous changes being brought about by the pandemic were better supported by a centralized versus decentralized procurement organization, and I would have the chance to build a centralized procurement organization from scratch. More specifically, I was uniquely positioned to create a Greenfield procurement organization that could build critical stakeholder relationships and develop strategic supplier relationships to maximize their competitive advantage and hopefully create potential savings opportunities.

I'm the type of person who prefers a challenge over following the status quo. During job interviews, I would not-so-jokingly say, "If you want to hire someone to row the boat, don't hire me. I want to put an outboard motor on the boat and make it go faster." During one of my interviews, the CIO simply said, "We don't have a boat, let us know what we need to do!"

Thinking back over ten plus years working in procurement, I realized I had implemented, or partially implemented, major procurement transformations by applying a common strategy that I called the Win-Win-Win approach to developing strategic supplier negotiations. But I was never offered a Greenfield opportunity and I always had to work within existing teams, existing processes, and existing multiple procurement to payment (P2P) technologies. This would be the first time I could actually start from scratch and leverage the key fundamentals that I had applied across multiple employers and procurement outsourcing clients over my career. What an exciting opportunity to build a new centralized global procurement organization from scratch!

Just like that, I started my new role and went from managing a global team of sixty-five people at Atos, to managing a team of zero (if you don't count me). My goal was to build and grow a procurement organization from scratch, but first I had to prove that my strategies worked. The Chief Operating Officer at the time, Sabina Rizvi, said, "Prove the value of procurement, and you can hire more people in the future."

By the end of the first six months, I was able to hire three additional people. It may not sound impressive, but because I was able to hire my own team, I chose people who had the same collaborative strategy as myself, one that focuses not just on our side winning, but a win for everyone involved. I was also able to work with legal, finance, security and data privacy to implement a process that better defined how our organizations collaborated together to meet our collective stakeholder needs. Collectively, we were able to focus on what was critical to the business and execute on the procurement opportunities we were able to generate. Although I was managing a smaller organization, our team was both strategic and effective; our processes were nimble and efficient and as a result we were able to manage significantly more projects and drive a higher savings percentage than I was typically able to deliver with my previous employers. At Accenture, Atos, or DXC, for instance, we had to work within the existing procurement structures and teams, and their processes were incredibly cumbersome. On average, my team would manage 10-15 projects per person, but today we are managing 20-25 projects per person. We were able to get our commercial negotiations completed in one month or less, whereas at other companies it may have taken several months to complete and obtain approval to proceed. As a result, we are incrementally increasing our value add from 7 percent to closer to 10 percent savings. I was able to do procurement my way, and it turns out my way is the winning strategy for everybody.

Throughout my career, I have worked in sales and in procurement. I have managed strategic supplier relationships with companies such as Google, Microsoft, Amazon, Oracle, Lenovo, Dell, HP—all the big players in the IT world. I've managed global Information Technology procurement teams as a procurement outsourcing consultant for companies like Electronic Data Systems, HP, Procurian, Farmers Insurance, Zurich Insurance, DXC, and Atos amongst others. I've managed accounts with up to $4.5 billion in spend. In short, I've led many global teams and have done a lot of complex global negotiations, but I have always taken a specific Win-Win-Win approach!

I didn't set out to do something "dramatically different" than everyone else; however, what I have discovered working across these companies is that the processes I have developed and implemented are in fact "dramatically different." Over the years I came to the conclusion that the pragmatic approach to establishing stakeholder relationships, developing strategic supplier relationships and conducting Win-Win-Win negotiation, although natural and intuitive to me, were not the industry standard. My first negotiation I was ever involved in, the customer and supplier were literally screaming at each other, and thinking back on that, I realized my approach wasn't common at all. Convinced I have found a much better way of doing things, I have advocated my Win-Win-Win approach, not only for myself and my teams, but also through discussions with supplier sales teams who manage multiple other strategic accounts.

The idea that I should write a book came to mind. If I'm doing things so differently—why not share my unique approach with the world?

In the following chapters you'll discover what ultimately forced me to refine my process into a collaborative procurement approach. Not only will you get my winning strategy, and a new approach to getting the best out of your negotiations, but by the time you're done reading this book you're going to have the skills to improve upon existing procurement processes, and organizational structure so that you can build your own procurement team (if you ever get the chance).

I didn't write this book only from a procurement perspective, and I didn't write it just for procurement people, there is valuable information in here for sales people, stakeholders, or anyone who uses or interacts with procurement and wants to better understand what procurement is trying to do. I wrote this book from the perspective of *all* the people who participate in a negotiation. The technology landscape is changing rapidly, and I am convinced the most collaborative will thrive, not just survive. Thanks for joining me, and I hope you enjoy the book!

Chapter 1
What is a Digital Metamorphosis?

"Today's market leader may not exist tomorrow, and tomorrow's market leader may not exist today." -Eric Dulin

If you're in procurement, you may have noticed over the last few years an industry-wide concept of what's known as a digital transformation, which is using digital to transform your business and the way it operates. Similar to how we moved from computers to tablets, to iPhones, to apps–the way people conduct business with companies has completely changed.

A recent Forbes article from February 2022 highlighted that a major global restaurant brand had set an industry development record and doubled digital sales in two years. The company mentioned had their sales reach $22 billion in fiscal 2021, an increase of 25 percent over 2020. This was not a small company. To suddenly drive 50 percent of revenue through digital channels in less than two years, is too fast and too dramatic to be a transformation. That's beyond transformation, that is a metamorphosis.

Before the pandemic, there wasn't an industry or business you could think of that didn't have some kind of app or mobile device capability. The restaurant industry had some of these in place, but technology was never the number one priority of most restaurants, it was serving food to their customers. But all that changed during the pandemic.

Do you remember going to your favorite restaurant on a Friday night and sitting down to dinner with the family? Do you remember when drive-thrus normally had a handful of cars in line and were only needed if you were eating on the run or taking food home to eat? But now, fast forward through pandemic times and lobbies were closed, there could be tens of people in line in the drive thru on any given day, and if you wanted to skip ahead, you had to use your new mobile app to order before you got in the queue or pick up from curbside. If you wanted to venture into the lobby, you could do so and there were minimal human contact options such as ordering through a kiosk. All of these IT solutions suddenly rocketed to the forefront during the pandemic to help you avoid the line and get your food quicker. It may have seemed like these things popped up overnight, but these technology solutions were already there in one form or another. The digital transformation was slowly changing the industry, but once the pandemic hit, technology suddenly sprang to the forefront of the restaurant industry. A transformation was no longer possible, a metamorphosis had to occur and it had to occur at light speed!

My cousin owns his own "mom and pop" restaurant, Dulin's Village Cafe in Vancouver, Washington. Like so many other mom and pop shops, he relied on his restaurant's location, food quality, friendly staff and reputation to drive business organically, as opposed to through a website, mobile application, drive through or delivery service. Like many other people in the restaurant industry, he struggled to go from dine-in to digital almost overnight. When COVID came, customers couldn't or didn't want to dine-in anymore, and my cousin was forced to close his lobby and switch to take out, call-in, or walk-in orders only. He launched a new website to stay abreast of the SEO changes happening on Google, and ran the kitchen himself, with only one server to help with the overflow. He didn't have the kitchen capacity to service all the walk-in customers and also do online ordering, he had to take the phone off the hook when they got busy. Thanks to the "Dulin fighting spirit," I'm proud to say my cousin was able to stay afloat financially during the entire pandemic without going into debt (although he may have thrown a few more swear words around than usual).

The Pace Has Accelerated

From a procurement standpoint, nothing is more exciting to me than the IT category. As we've seen with the businesses who survived the pandemic, technology touches everything that a company does, from managing their sales, operations, product development and services processes to managing their corporate functions. As we look back on the past few years (a decade is too long) a lot has changed. The pace of innovation has increased dramatically. The speed of technological advancement and the ability to expand new concepts using cloud infrastructure and the availability of capital have created a vortex of new technology companies. Tech startup companies are being created every day, companies are being acquired at an unprecedented rate, and many businesses that aren't able to keep up with the pace of change are falling by the wayside. Another interesting consequence of this new digital marketplace is the fact that a new company's strategic advantages decrease rapidly over time as other companies copy their business model and leverage improved technology infrastructure to launch competing firms.

The late Pierre Nanterme, former CEO of Accenture, summed up Digital Transformation when he said, "Digital is redefining the way we work every day, presenting a profound challenge for business leaders to rethink almost everything about how their organizations operate. Indeed, the race to transform into a digital business is a massive responsibility for leaders, but it's also an important opportunity for companies to reinvent themselves."

A digital metamorphosis is a digital transformation on steroids.

Kiosks are a good example of a digital metamorphosis done correctly. Pre-pandemic you may have noticed a few kiosks here and there, or some self-checkout lanes in grocery stores for those who were willing to take a self-directed path. Kiosks may not have changed your life that much, but in reality they were a revolutionary solution for the industry to reduce labor costs and support customers. From a team member standpoint, each member of the team can now focus more of their time on food production and restaurant and store operations versus order taking. And from a customer standpoint, kiosks also eliminate errors, as the customer could validate the order before hitting send. Now in pandemic times, with increased labor shortages in all industries, kiosks have become critical to manage customer flow through stores and restaurants. That person who used to take orders is now preparing the orders and helping customers get in and out even faster, and precious labor is redirected to other more important parts of the business. As a side note, as a customer during my last trip to my local super Walmart, there were no cashier lanes–there are now twenty plus self-checkout lanes! And one bored Guest Services person managing the entire front end of the store by occasionally responding to a flashing light. Times have changed.

The reality is a lot of preparation goes into making a successful digital metamorphosis. Like the book cover shows, the digital metamorphosis accelerates the process; there is no egg, there is no cocoon, there is no time. A caterpillar turns into a butterfly instantly. The digital channels either have been created and need to be scaled, or need to be created in the first place, and sales will exponentially accelerate through the channels. Businesses have to create the tools, conduct testing, and optimize the channels and most importantly, they have to leverage a new ability to gather customer data and market analytics, and refine a marketing plan based on infinitely more information than ever before. Whether you acquire the solution, develop the solution yourself, hire someone else to build it, or some combination of the three–it's a lot to do in a small amount of time. That's the challenge of a digital metamorphosis! The table below shows some of the critical areas of focus from the past two years.

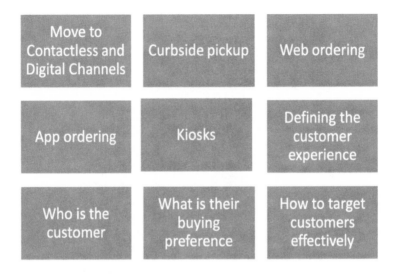

Move to Contactless and Digital Channels	Curbside pickup	Web ordering
App ordering	Kiosks	Defining the customer experience
Who is the customer	What is their buying preference	How to target customers effectively

Collaboration Is An Advantage

As we've witnessed with the restaurant industry, COVID-19 forced many businesses to dramatically change the way they operate to include the immediate need for digital capabilities. Our customers' needs totally changed, and our response had to change as well. This goes well beyond the digital transformation that many companies were embarking on prior to COVID.

Another key phenomenon of the digital metamorphosis was the ability for companies to design and build their own software solution. In the old days, when you needed a supplier it was as easy as looking at supplier A, B, C, and thinking—*what do they have and what can best meet my needs*? Today, you're looking at supplier A, B and C and saying—*I need to create a solution to do something different. What do they have that I can add to my ecosystem of solution providers to help me get what I need? Or, how can they help me build something that doesn't exist yet?*

There have historically been three options to obtaining a software solution. One, purchase a single integrated product that best meets your needs. Two, purchase multiple components of an overall solution and integrate them together. Three, build your own software solution. Through advances in agile technology, software development technology, software development tools and Application Protocol Interfaces, the ability to develop your own software is much less daunting than it was in the past. The challenge now is finding the right talent to help design and build your product. In the Information Technology and Software Development industry, talent is in demand! The dramatic shift to work-from-home and non-traditional working models have made access to more talent readily available, but the competition to attract and retain the top talent is incredibly difficult.

The talent shortage coupled with the need to move quickly is leading to a hybrid model of the "buy and build." Companies are adopting a "make and buy" strategy and using their talent and resources to develop the critical core components of a software product. Then they add additional capabilities from existing products, where possible, to obtain speed to market and cost effectiveness while implementing new software products.

The digital metamorphosis companies are undergoing today requires procurement and suppliers to rethink their strategies to develop the strategic relationships critical to defining a company's competitive advantage in the marketplace. Procurement and strategic suppliers both need to understand this shift in relationship management and align their strategic objectives to help their joint customers succeed in creating these competitive advantages. Companies themselves need to rethink their technology strategy and move away from independent business entity specific strategies and align on future technology solutions that support both the good of the individual business and the good of the parent company.

When negotiating third party supplier agreements to support digital go-to market offerings for Accenture or when developing custom client outsourcing solutions for DXC or Atos, oftentimes the suppliers we hired were building solutions for us like big data offerings, e-commerce platforms, or other custom solutions. It was also common for us to find different, often competing, vendors and integrate them together into a common portfolio of suppliers that could be mixed and matched to respond to a client proposal to solve a digital problem. We created collaborative, cooperation-based relationships where otherwise normally competing vendors participated as part of an integrated solution portfolio to pursue and win new business.

This portfolio of suppliers is developed under a standard set of terms, conditions and Service Level Agreements (SLAs) with pre-negotiated pricing so that the only negotiation required is with the client to win the business. The solution architect analyzes the problem, identifies the required solution, prices the proposal. and presents the proposal within 3-5 business days. The suppliers have resources available to start the engagement within 1-2 weeks. This integrated network of suppliers collaborating to solve identified client opportunities has driven millions of dollars of business for multiple sales teams. Today, the right "ecosystem" of suppliers can help you get what you need done as efficiently and as cost-effectively as possible.

In short, if you want to lead a successful metamorphosis you must have the right partnerships with the right suppliers in place, and if you want a competitive advantage in the new digital world, you must focus on collaboration.

Now that we've explored how digital metamorphosis is impacting procurement, in the next chapter we'll be exploring why procurement fails, and how you can prevent your stakeholders from straying.

Chapter 2
Going From Administrative Obstruction to Trusted Advisor

"When procurement enables us as a true partner, it allows us to be honest and real about our needs–the details, the urgency, the risk areas– and then the team can deliver a program and construct that gets us on the best path with the supplier." -Sasha W. VP Marketing

One time I had a chief Information Security Officer (CISO) for one of my procurement outsourcing clients come to me with an incredibly challenging request. He had received a larger amount of unforecasted end-of-year budget and had been asked to use it to shore up his company's security. He'd completed a rapid risk assessment and identified about twenty-five suppliers that he needed to complete negotiations with, but the catch was, he had to complete them before the end of the year. He said, "I've got twenty-five deals that I've got to get done by December, otherwise I'm going to lose the end of year money." This was the middle of November.

He paused for a second and then added, "Look, there is no way that you and your team can get this done. It's okay. Go ahead and tell me now so that I can pay for someone else to come in and complete these negotiations. I have to get them done."

I said, "That's ok, I can get them done."

He repeated, "You can't get them done. It's okay. Tell me now, and I'll bring someone in."

I said, "No, I'll make it happen. I'll check in with you weekly to review the status."

He had zero confidence in me, but I was determined to get these deals done. I immediately pulled in half a dozen resources from legal and procurement and dedicated them to completing the contracts. Because we were short on time, we adopted a "get the yes" approach. What that basically meant was, from a legal standpoint, we only focused on absolutely critical contractual clauses that prevented us from negotiating a deal such as limitation of liability, indemnification, intellectual property rights, and so on. We told the legal team, "We can't negotiate everything, we need to focus on critical contractual clauses that are preventing us from signing the deal."

Next, we informed the vendors they had to accept our company's contracts if they wanted to get this done. Then we went to the commercial team and asked them to do extremely aggressive price negotiations, and to complete them in three rounds.

By the first weekly check in with my client, we had completed four of the agreements. Needless to say he was surprised. That was the last status meeting we ever had regarding the project. From that point forward I didn't have to meet with him anymore, I just sent him weekly status reports. By the end of December, we had closed all but three or four of the major agreements. The ones we hadn't closed were due to the supplier's unwillingness to "get to yes" and accept the required terms and conditions. This was understood by the client, and they accepted they weren't going to close.

The reason I was able to exceed this CISO's expectations is that over time I've learned there are three critical obstructions that cause procurement to fail, and what made those negotiations successful is that I had taken every step to prevent them from occurring. Those three things are:

1. We don't understand what's important to a customer. We'll spend hours debating legal terms and conditions, and weeks negotiating pricing, when all the customer is really concerned about is being able to sign the contract so they can start their project on time. From a procurement outsourcing perspective, oftentimes, when we examined our relationships with our clients and our renewal percentages, what we found is that even though we hit our savings targets almost 100 percent of the time, a significant percentage of our clients did not renew our services. What that means is that our clients did not renew because they weren't happy with how we provided our procurement services; we didn't understand what was important to them.

Recently, I had the opportunity to support multiple procurement outsourcing clients where I took over an existing account mid-stream. Unfortunately, every client was a red client which meant that they were not happy with the service we provided. After meeting with Directors, Senior VPs and CIOs, what I discovered was that we weren't building our relationships with our stakeholders. Instead of proactively engaging with our customers to understand their business challenges, their need to leverage technology to solve that business challenge, and ultimately working with them to develop a technology roadmap and procurement project pipeline, we were simply waiting for the clients to come to us with a discrete project portfolio. We were not taking the time to understand their needs or how their specific needs fit into the overall strategy. Once the client approached us, we would assign a highly competent procurement negotiator to negotiate the deal, however, they also didn't understand the client's success criteria.

The CIO who was obligated to deliver that service within their defined budget or the project manager who was obligated to deliver the project within their defined timeframe was not concerned about saving money. They just needed the project delivered on time. Many times we allowed projects to be delayed by extensive commercial or legal negotiations, which means we won the negotiation with the supplier but lost our stakeholders and ultimately our clients.

2. Stakeholders feel the procurement process is too cumbersome. One of the biggest challenges we face in procurement is that the procurement process itself is incredibly complex, lengthy, and in all honesty, not 100 percent owned by procurement. The end-to-end procurement processes take too long, we get caught up in minutiae and we can't meet stakeholder deadlines. We will be addressing this more in later chapters, and you will get some tips on streamlining your process. In the meantime, on to the next roadblock.

3. Stakeholders feel the procurement person doesn't understand their product or service. This goes hand-in-hand with not taking the time to build a relationship with your stakeholders, and establishing trust. In some cases, stakeholders are intimately familiar with their specific needs, with the suppliers that provide those specific services, and any changes happening in that specific industry. If that is the stakeholder's full job responsibility and therefore all they do, they are deep specialists in that area of expertise. In some cases, the stakeholder may not understand the industry at all and may need help determining who the right suppliers are to even consider. Additionally, those same subject matter experts are not procurement resources. They are not used to facilitating a procurement project and are not used to conducting comprehensive supplier evaluations to make informed decisions. The big challenge for procurement, in either case, is learning how to integrate both sets of knowledge into a successful procurement project.

These three obstructions are further exacerbated by the procurement policies of companies. Some companies have an enforced mandate that all significant third party purchases must be conducted by procurement and even that spend above a certain value must be competitively bid. Other companies are much more lax on their policy and delegate procurement decisions to directors or above. Depending on the procurement policy and the perception of the stakeholder, if there are alternatives to procurement, the causes above, especially number two and three, may cause a stakeholder to abandon procurement support and try to negotiate the contracts themselves, regardless of the company's procurement mandate. In my opinion, procurement is a failure when either the stakeholder doesn't come to procurement and negotiates the agreement on their own or when procurement is engaged to support the stakeholder, but misses one of the five success criteria that we will discuss in the next section.

Why was that CISO so adamant I couldn't succeed? One, he was absolutely convinced that we wouldn't be able to meet his timeframe requirements. Two, he didn't feel we would have the knowledge to execute the procurement activity, our team didn't have the expertise—only *his team* had that ability. Three, he also knew our process was cumbersome and did not believe we could modify the process to meet his critical time frame. Lastly, his company had a procurement mandate, but he wanted me to admit defeat so he could circumvent procurement for those reasons.

Understand Your Value

Early in my procurement outsourcing career, I scheduled a meeting with the client's Chief Information Officer. I spent the day preparing for the meeting. In true procurement fashion, I reviewed their technology spend, broke the spend down into categories and subcategories, and then looked at each of the major suppliers in each subcategory to identify potential savings opportunities. I then applied our procurement savings estimates to determine how much money I would be able to save. I then spent an hour putting together some great charts to explain what those opportunities and savings were. I felt extremely prepared for the meeting and confident that I could demonstrate the value that we would bring as a procurement outsourcing partner.

I arrived at his office on time, introduced myself, sat down across from him and handed him his copy of the presentation so we could begin the discussion. To my surprise, he quickly flipped through the deck, glanced briefly to each slide, and then turned around and tossed the presentation (and all my hard work) into the trash. He then looked at me and said the keywords that I will never forget, "I want you to be a help to my team."

What a profound statement. For a procurement person, especially a procurement outsourcing person, I was paid to, and judged by, my ability to deliver savings. But this CIO did not care about savings. What he cared about was the fact that he had to meet his obligations to provide technology services to the business, and his team were far more concerned about managing the project timeline within the project budget, than saving money by reducing the project budget.

This one conversation forever changed my perspective of what procurement value is. I clearly understood that *business engagement* was critical to success, but I now knew that success was based on how effectively I met the stakeholder requirements versus how well I delivered cost savings. In order to prove my value, I had to know my stakeholders and understand what their priorities were and take a customer service approach to managing their expectations. Managing expectations included knowing and providing project management insight to the end-to-end procurement process. I had to ensure I collaboratively defined the journey the stakeholders were about to embark on to complete the supplier negotiation, keep them updated during the journey, and ensure that we stayed on track to meet the collective timeline!

To accomplish this then, and forever in the future, I had to engage with all members of the end-to-end procurement process (legal, security, data privacy, supplier setup, etc.) so that there was a defined vision, project plan, and R.A.C.I. (Responsible, Accountable, Consult and Inform) matrix for each critical negotiation. We documented the process and created a project plan template for all future projects and used it for critical strategic negotiations going forward. This template was then used to set expectations and define project timelines with the internal team initially and then with the supplier when negotiations began in earnest–a template is an incredible tool to both set and manage expectations as well as manage project timelines!

Working in procurement outsourcing has given me the opportunity to work with a myriad of companies in multiple industries including biotechnology, service, manufacturing, consumer products, and insurance. This multi-company perspective clearly illustrated the difference between when procurement was viewed as an "administrative obstruction," and when procurement was viewed as a "trusted advisor." The difference is that when you're an administrative roadblock, you're simply viewed as the person responsible for ensuring the contract is signed by the right people during a negotiation. And when you're a "trusted advisor," you are working to understand the stakeholder's challenges, and helping to identify potential solutions to their business problems, then finding the right third party supplier who can deliver that solution. Obviously, I prefer the latter arrangement and when you build this relationship with stakeholders, they are more than willing to relinquish the procurement responsibility to someone who actually wants to do it.

Five Keys For Success

From that point on, I was able to come up with five criteria for the success of procurement, and those criteria are; 1) define the right requirements for the business; 2) select the right supplier to deliver the products and services needed to meet the business need; and 3) at the right price and; 4) within the right time frame to meet the business need. (Yes, I know that's only four, the fifth one will be explained shortly.)

Recently, we negotiated a project for our marketing team where the stakeholders had been negotiating with a company for almost a year. They had not completed the negotiation and were becoming somewhat frustrated. They engaged my team and one of my senior sourcing managers and we took a more strategic approach. Instead of negotiating for a couple of countries for two business units, we elevated the opportunity to a global negotiation for all business units. Although we increased the complexity, we were able to finalize the initial negotiation within two months and achieved a significantly better outcome than the stakeholder expected. We were then able to complete additional negotiations to address other countries as well. Our stakeholder was so excited that she invited us to attend a marketing leadership meeting and discuss what we were able to achieve. We attended that meeting and presented what we had done and we were instantly rewarded with several additional projects in the marketing space, a category which had been "taboo" for procurement to support in the past.

Successfully executing a procurement project is actually not the end goal, as I'm sure you noticed. The end goal is delighting your stakeholder and creating an advocate that is willing to recommend you to their peers and executives so that you can provide great customer service to them!

As a procurement person, I have always been measured on procurement Value Add (savings and cost avoidance); however, I consider this to be a byproduct of stakeholder collaboration and effectively solving stakeholder challenges, not the primary focus. I am still expected to complete a savings forecast and set my annual savings targets, however, once those targets are set, I focus almost entirely on stakeholder engagement and stakeholder collaboration. The *true* measure and finally the fifth measure of procurement success is; 5) create a stakeholder advocate that will recommend procurement to their peers. The additional projects, spend, and saving opportunities are ultimately what helps us meet our savings needs.

In short, use the chart below to get to know your stakeholder's needs and build trust with them. You will never be viewed as an administrative roadblock again.

Who are my Stakeholders?

What are Their Priorities?

How do Their Needs Align with the Company?

What are their Expectations?

How do we collaborate to Drive Successful Procurement?

Chapter 3
Wooing Your Stakeholders

One year, we had a software company approach three different CIOs and senior VPs at my procurement outsourcing client and solicit three independent software sales. Normally, at the end of the year, sales teams go and pursue clients to try and drive new business. This supplier sales team had been extremely successful in offering end of year deals and each business unit was interested in making an independent investment and essentially an independent purchase. The problem was that each of those three executives were only focused on their own independent deals, they only cared about their own project, and weren't interested in bundling their project in with the others.

There was a huge opportunity to bundle the spend and drive a consolidated savings opportunity, however, I had the added challenge of completing the supplier negotiations at light speed and being able to contract and sign in a matter of one to two weeks. In my discussion with each of the business unit VPs, I was specifically told that their project was "critical," it had to be completed by year's end and therefore could not be bundled with other projects and slowed down. The reality was, if we consolidated the deal we could get much better pricing, but they were more concerned about timing, not pricing.

Ultimately, I had to escalate this to the client's Chief Procurement Officer and he gave me permission to negotiate this as a consolidated deal instead of three separate projects. Then I met with each senior VP and got their buy-in to consolidate the purchase and complete the negotiation by mid-December (with a little persuasion from the client's CPO). We were able to complete an aggressive consolidated negotiation, and by bundling the purchases into a single consolidated purchase, and completing the negotiation at the supplier's year end, we were able to achieve almost 50 percent savings off the individual supplier offers. Obtaining the stakeholder buy-in and trust enabled my team to drive great savings opportunities for our client.

The moral of the story is that you must convince your stakeholders to trust and empower you. You have to convince them that you understand what's important to them and you're going to get their project accomplished. They have to *believe* you and trust you, otherwise they'll go do it themselves. This chapter is what I have learned over the course of my career about wooing your stakeholders and earning their trust.

Conversely, when I worked on my first sales opportunity for IBM, I made the mistake of negotiating a supplier agreement without engaging procurement. I was politely informed that this was not only against the rules, but that is a fireable offense! Fortunately for me, initial mistakes were forgiven and I was not at all interested in repeating my mistakes.

Throughout my procurement career, I have worked for companies that had clearly enforced procurement policies and mandates, policies that were not enforced (I call this "recommended reading" policies) and no procurement policies at all (the proverbial Wild, Wild West). The challenge, even in companies with mandated procurement involvement, was when the stakeholders engaged procurement. In some cases the stakeholder negotiated with the business and engaged procurement at a transactional level solely to "process the paperwork." My goal when leading procurement organizations was to become strategic procurement and be engaged by stakeholders when they first contemplated buying something and ultimately to assist them in facilitating the procurement process from the very beginning. Mandate or no mandate, this only happens by taking the correct customer service approach, with the attitude of, "I am procurement, how can I help you?"

Get Aligned

"The Win-Win-Win model is, by far, the best strategy when aligning with procurement teams. This approach ensures alignment, enables all stakeholders to enjoy success, and gets every team rowing in the same direction." -Mitch Schneider, Strategic Account Executive (Sales), Braze

I cannot think of many procurement projects that are executed for the benefit of one individual stakeholder. In today's world of complex global companies, with multiple brands, multiple business units and multiple business functions, aligning sets of stakeholders to a common goal is the first and most critical step in any procurement activity. In most cases, misalignment occurs because stakeholders are simply concerned about "their project" or "their timeline" and not necessarily concerned about everyone else.

The first step that I take to prepare for a negotiation is simply to anticipate the stakeholder alignment discussions and what the various party objections will be. Stakeholders are incented to support both their business unit and company objectives; however, aligning them to take the same negotiation or strategic supplier path can be difficult. By anticipating these, I can be prepared to discuss the benefits of a consolidated negotiations and why those outweigh the cons. In some cases, due to where they are in the digital metamorphosis journey, or resource constraints, the optimal outcome may in fact be different supplier solutions for the various stakeholder groups; however, acknowledging that up front alleviates stakeholder concerns. Another big objection may be transition requirements to move to a consolidated vendor. Again that should be acknowledged up front and considered in the overall business case. I am always prepared to escalate to senior leadership if I need to; however, by properly anticipating and addressing potential stakeholder concerns, that is a very rare occurrence and happens less than 1 percent of the time.

Define, Define, Define

Defining the procurement strategy itself is another challenge for stakeholder alignment. For example, I worked in a federal consulting practice for a major global consulting company. During my tenure there, we competed for the renewal of a major department of defense contract that we were the prime vendor on. As part of our sales pursuit plan, we began working months prior to the renewal to identify the key decision makers that would be involved in the RFP process/program management and governance. We looked for opportunities to understand their perspective on the competitive landscape and our probability of winning, and learn what we needed to do to influence them to ensure we retained the business.

Not every sales team goes to this extreme, however the sales team's goal is to try to win the business without engaging in the expense of responding to an RFP, especially if the client's procurement policy does not mandate competitive bidding. In those cases, the sales team engages directly with the business stakeholders to convince them that their product is the best in the market and that they can provide that amazing product for an even more amazing price.

This creates challenges with stakeholders who may feel that their exposure to that one product has given them the ability to make an informed decision or may otherwise feel that due to circumstances (timing, speed to market, end of year budget), they do not have time to undertake a long and arduous RFP process.

By clarifying that the goal of an RFP is to provide the stakeholder the best possible information needed to make a decision and agreeing to complete the RFP within a reasonable timeframe that aligns to the stakeholder expectations, most business stakeholders will be willing (although occasionally begrudgingly) to support the RFP process.

Ask For It

Another interesting phenomenon that I have discovered while at-tempting to gain stakeholder alignment is that sometimes it is as simple as asking for it. When I took over the procurement organization for one company, I met with multiple IT stakeholders across the different busi-ness units. During an introductory one-on-one, one of the many stake-holders (a Director of IT) said, *"I'm glad you are here, now you can help us align our technology stacks."*

This was an incredibly ironic statement to me based on my experience working in multiple technology companies. Procurement does not nor-mally *define* the architecture; we wait for technology governance to *define* the technology architecture so that procurement can *negotiate* it. I thought to myself, *I don't have the skills to make technology deci-sions, but there is currently an absence of a formal technology govern-ance program. How can I collaborate with my stakeholders (who have all of the necessary skills) and provide them a forum that allows them to analyze the options and make a decision?*

First, I had to determine who the key stakeholders were across the re-spective business units and create a stakeholder matrix of key stake-holders. As my relationship base expanded and new stakeholders were defined, they were added to the group. What originally started at about twenty-five stakeholders tripled in size and now includes legal, finance, security, risk and data privacy. (With any group of this size, over-com-munication is better than under-communication!)

Next, I created a mailing group so that I could keep those key stake-holders informed of new projects. When stakeholders engaged with me to support a new project, I added it to a weekly note that was sent to the key stakeholder distribution list to inform them of the new pro-jects that were coming up and ask them to determine which stakehold-ers wanted to participate on each project. The project was also added to our procurement project tracking sheet which is a shared document that all stakeholders have access to. When individual stakeholders notified me or the team that they were interested in a specific project, they were added to the spreadsheet as the representatives for their respective business unit.

Procurement is one of the few organizations that has complete visibility of the critical business initiatives that are happening across all business units. The challenge is that there is seldom an effective communication tool for informing stakeholders of the projects that are happening, engaging the right stakeholders on the projects that they are interested in, and keeping them informed of that project status. This simple communication process can become a great tool to inform stakeholders and gain wider acceptance by the business units.

Once I had identified individual projects and had key stakeholders defined for each business unit, the next step in developing collaboration was to define the company technology strategy and determine the procurement approach. Each business unit representative was responsible for understanding what their business unit was doing today, their desired future approach, and the strengths and weaknesses of both their current and future approach. During the kickoff meetings, each stakeholder met with other interested stakeholders to discuss their perspectives and align on the desired approach(es) to take. I was pleasantly surprised with the results that occurred when the different business units met to discuss the suppliers they were using, the challenges they faced, and their willingness to accept alternative suppliers. Collaboration had been established.

Another example of when stakeholder collaboration was incredibly effective was during a brand management supplier negotiation for multiple business units. When companies operate different brands, there are cases where suppliers look at each brand independently instead of viewing each brand as part of the same company. This is further exacerbated when the businesses are geographically dispersed and the supplier companies assign multiple sales teams to work with stakeholders at each location. In this particular negotiation, each business unit had its own contract and pricing based on their individual business unit volume versus the company's aggregate total volume. Not only were we not optimizing aggregate volume, but we were also actually all paying different prices for the same service across the different business units. It was not the ideal contract structure.

To remedy the situation, first I engaged with the supplier and requested a consolidated price based on our total cumulative enterprise volume, including forecasted growth and explained that I expected our overall price to decrease due to the increased spend amount and that it should be cheaper than our current best price. They agreed to provide a price and I was incredibly dismayed when the total cumulative price they proposed was actually higher than the aggregate price we were paying.

Increasing our cost, as our spend volume increases, directly conflicts with the Win-Win-Win strategy, which we will discuss in future chapters, but as a result of this price increase, the supplier themselves set the conditions for a competitive bid. My challenge was that this was an incumbent supplier that all of the business units were using, so I was not sure it would be possible to convince the business to competitively bid this opportunity. Fortunately, multiple cost-effective suppliers existed in the market, the supplier was increasing prices and the stakeholders had some concerns about their overall performance. I went to the stakeholders and requested that we competitively bid and fortunately, they agreed, and we invited multiple suppliers to bid! Thanks to the stakeholders incredible willingness to competitively bid this opportunity, and the competitive pressure created, the price of the overall solution was significantly reduced. We basically gave the incumbent supplier the ultimatum to provide a market competitive price or lose all the business. We ended up renewing with the incumbent supplier at a significant reduction because a reduced percentage of the business was better than 0 percent.

Over time, and through multiple negotiations, I identified stakeholder groups that consistently met to negotiate similar supplier agreements for specific areas of expertise such as testing or marketing technology (MARTEC). Based on these "repeat customers," I established cross business unit Centers of Excellence (COEs) for each of the major technology stack components and then invited members of each of the business units to participate in those COEs. The topics extended well beyond supplier negotiations to sharing best practices and establishing technology roadmaps. My goal for these COEs once the major supplier negotiations have been completed is to transition those over to the business to run and manage.

During one testing COE meeting the team discussed testing suppliers that they were using. One business unit was not happy with their incumbent supplier and was interested in moving to an alternate supplier, a second business unit was already using the alternate supplier but was also unhappy with them, a third business unit was considering a completely different supplier, and ultimately through the collaborative discussion, the three business units evaluated and ultimately moved to the third supplier. Without the COE to facilitate this discussion, multiple sub-optimal decisions may have been made.

Good Governance

In addition to establishing this informal technology architecture process, I have worked collaboratively with multiple business units to establish a formal technology governance process. Each business unit has their own technology stack today. The first step in establishing the technology architecture process was defining the current state of each business unit. We collaboratively created a spreadsheet that listed the technology stack components (including security) as rows. We then listed each business unit as a column and the business units filled out the technology components in their respective column. This created a view of the comprehensive technology landscape that we had in place today. This also provided incredible value to the procurement team because it identified multiple consolidation opportunities.

First, it identified cases where we had a single technology provider that had individually contracted with multiple business units. In one case, I identified that multiple brands were using the same analytics reseller; however, that reseller was not actually a preferred supplier partner. I engaged with the OEM and was able to find multiple preferred resellers. By conducting a competitive bid across the incumbent and two preferred resellers, we were able to Procure more product for a significantly cheaper price than what the incumbent supplier offered.

Additionally, this view also defined cases where we used different suppliers to provide the same solution and highlighted opportunities to consolidate suppliers. An example is a technology service performance tracking software vendor. We originally consolidated our spend into a single aggregate global agreement instead of a multi-business unit agreement, however, as part of that negotiation, the decision was made to ultimately move away from that supplier. We identified and signed an agreement with a different supplier. Due to the timing of each business unit's migration and existing contract expiration, we were not able to renew for all business units simultaneously. Instead, to support our end state migration as defined in our technology roadmap, we negotiated a tiered pricing agreement with the new supplier based on the initial business unit spend and included pricing tiers structured to support additional future business unit migrations. Currently, our agreement and discounts are negotiated and all we have to do now is focus on executing the transition from the old suppliers and migration to the new supplier upon expiration of the current agreements.

End to end, what does it mean to manage your stakeholders effectively? For one, they are willing to collaborate and aren't operating autonomously. Also, ideally, there is a technology architecture governance in place, people can't just go out and buy whatever they want. Lastly, to be effective, governance must be enforced. Governance with 100 percent approval of exception requests is not governance; in effective governance, some things get denied. The opposite is a "recommended reading policy" and it doesn't work.

Renewals

Speaking of technology governance, renewals are a good time to look at technology governance. You shouldn't just arbitrarily renew your agreement without taking time to confirm that it aligns with your technology governance and what you're trying to do. It's the only time you have a chance to swap something out, especially if you work across multiple business units. There's always an opportunity to renew that agreement and bundle that with more spend. For example, I recently negotiated an agreement with a supplier where we had one business using the product currently, but their current agreement was about to expire and was up for renewal; another business was already using the supplier, but they weren't up for renewal for several months; and a third business that was interested in signing a new agreement. We basically bundled all of the deals together, negotiated a renewal for the first business unit, an early renewal for the second business unit, and a new purchase for the third business unit, which was a much better consolidated purchase than we would have done as three independent renewals.

Define Exceptions

Once global standards are defined, there will always be a need to seek and obtain approval for exceptions to that standard! In Solution Integrator companies, for example, there are always going to be customer related requirements that demand an alternative solution. This could be due to differences in customer owned technology stacks or the need to interface with or support other technologies. Regardless of the reason, the architecture governance exception process needs to provide both the standards required for any non-standard solution to meet, as well as the process to request and approve an exception.

The technology exception standards should be the same as the standards that are met by the global standard technology vendors and should also include critical considerations such as single sign on, SLA requirements, technology requirements, etc. Both the global standards and the technology standards should be defined by the business' technology teams.

The process to request and obtain technology governance acceptance should be defined by business leadership and should in fact be a true process where decisions are made, and exception requests are sometimes not approved. I have worked for companies where the exception governance process never denied an exception request which meant there was really no exception process. Exceptions that meet the technical requirements and make business sense should be approved.

Working with the business to establish cross functional teams and Centers of Excellence, (of communication), Standard Suppliers with, (Technology Exception Standards and Technology Exception Approvals) is the ultimate in procurement and stakeholder collaboration! Establishing this basic fundamental process prior to starting supplier negotiations is the ultimate in procurement optimization since it defines the technology roadmap and creates the ability for procurement to plan for and engage in upcoming supplier negotiations.

Now that you understand how to woo your stakeholders, let's dive into the key tenets of the Win-Win-Win strategy!

Chapter 4
The Win-Win-Win Strategy

"If you know the enemy and know yourself you need not fear the results of a hundred battles." -Sun Tzu

If you are familiar with the classic business strategy book *The Art of War*, this ties into the quote from Sun Tzu that I shared above. As a former Armored Cavalry Officer and "military" leader, this meant that I needed to understand the capabilities of my team, the capabilities of my enemy, and if I did not have sufficient resources to win the battle, to wait and continue to add force multipliers until I had the ability to engage and defeat the enemy. From a procurement standpoint, I would rephrase this quote to say, "If you understand what the stakeholder, the supplier, and procurement need in order to achieve a successful negotiation, you don't need to fear the results of any negotiation."

The Win-Win-Win strategy is focused on understanding the perspectives of all the participants in a negotiation and defines—what a win for the supplier, a win for the business, and a win for procurement look like—so that you can best align to come to an agreement for all parties. The Win-Win-Win strategy ultimately starts with a **win for the business** by establishing a relationship and signing contractual and commercial agreements that allow them to buy the products and services they need easily and efficiently. Essentially both procurement and the supplier negotiate to be a help to the business team!

The second **win is for the supplier**. If procurement and the supplier negotiate an effective agreement then ideally the business will use the suppliers' products, and spend more money which will drive more revenue for the supplier. This can happen by expanding the products and scope of services you purchase, offering products and services to other business units, looking for competitive displacement of other supplier products or procuring products and services for longer time periods.

The third **win is for procurement** (from a measurement standpoint only). Ideally, by negotiating volume-based tiered contracts established on anticipated growth. As supplier revenue increases, they are able to offer lower costs per unit which results in savings for procurement. In large global corporations, these lower unit costs may unlock other international markets and encourage even more supplier spend and adoption.

There is also a fourth win as well that applies when the business is actually selling or offering a product or service to their **end customer** and as the cost of their ultimate product or service decreases, they can extend that lower pricing to those customers.

The Key Tenets Of Negotiation

During a kickoff meeting with one of my Latin America teams, we had an external procurement and negotiation consultant talk about negotiations. One of the things he said that ultimately did not resonate with me was that when he was preparing for a negotiation, he felt a little anxious in the pit of his stomach. Anxiety is something I may have had in the very first couple of negotiations, but fundamentally if you look at what a negotiation is and what you are trying to achieve from a Win-Win-Win approach, anxiety indicates that you are taking the wrong approach!

I have been fortunate enough to work in both sales and procurement and I have also been both the customer stakeholder and the supplier delivery team lead responsible for delivering the results of the negotiated agreement to the customer stakeholder. By having had the opportunity to sit at every chair around the negotiation table, I have realized that there are a few basic tenets that all negotiations will follow and that if you understand those tenets, and you propose the Win-Win-Win approach, you can execute each negotiation successfully. Therefore, I do not walk into a negotiation feeling anxious, but instead walk into a negotiation feeling confident and excited that the negotiation team will achieve a successful outcome.

The key tenets to consider and understand about the negotiation are:

Tenet 1: You are on the same team trying to achieve the same result. Too many people fail to realize that both the supplier and procurement want to achieve the same result from a negotiation: a negotiated agreement between the company and the supplier. If you look at the definition of the procurement success and slightly modify the definition to see it from the sales team's perspective you get a definition of: *working with the business and ultimately **procurement** to; a) identify the right requirements; b) **prove that I am** the right supplier to deliver the products and services needed to meet the business need; c) at the right price and; d) within the right time frame to meet the business need.* You can even agree that the supplier would love to have the stakeholder become an advocate for them and present them to their peers and/or leadership.

There are several points of contention in this first tenet which immediately appear to create conflict between procurement and the supplier. One point is price and the second is the terms and conditions of the agreement. In both cases, the expectation is that each party will seek out the most favorable pricing and most favorable terms and conditions for their respective party; however, there are a couple of other tenets to consider...

Tenet 2: No company is expected to negotiate for a position that causes them to lose money. Notice that Tenet 1 states "at the right price." Right price is key here. It is not about charging an infinite amount of money or about negotiating for the absolute lowest price, nor is it simply a supply and demand equals market price. If I define the right price from a procurement standpoint, it would be a price for a product or service that is benchmarked to be competitive with other competitors in the market and other suppliers whose solution delivers similar value. The price should enable the business to deliver a **sufficiently positive ROI** for the benefits they are expected to receive from implementing the product or service. If I look at price from a supplier standpoint, I would define it as the price at which I will recover my costs to deliver the product or service, obtain a profitable margin and be able to provide a **sufficiently positive ROI** to my customer. I italicized and bolded positive ROI to point out that neither a supplier nor the stakeholder/procurement should be willing to sign a deal that does not add value to the customer, the same customer—so in essence, both teams should be looking to find that price. If the price is too high, alternative suppliers will be selected, if the price is too low, the supplier will not be willing or able to meet that price, therefore, the price should work itself out through the competitive bidding and market intelligence process.

The interesting thing that I have discovered through running multiple global negotiations is that, frequently, the right price varies geographically. For example, I was in a negotiation with a deep linking and mobile attribution company. During the negotiation, they presented a pricing model that was consistent for each country across the globe, but unfortunately the model had multiple issues that had to be resolved. First and foremost, their initial cost of their overall product compared with the value add of the product was prohibitive. In many smaller global countries, their product cost *more* than the cost to implement the mobile application that they would be improving or even the eCommerce platform being used for online ordering in that country.

To achieve the right price, we had to develop regional pricing to align their product value with the other products in the market. From a supplier standpoint, the cost to develop a product to support the US, UK, or other major international country was significantly higher than the cost to develop a product to support India or a smaller international country; therefore, their right price had to be higher in some countries than others. The resulting and somewhat complex pricing model was essentially a regional/country specific pricing model that was negotiated at the global level but considered the country specific nuances and pricing in each country. The supplier was able to offer a "right price" that made their product competitive in each of the local markets.

Tenet 3: No company is expected to negotiate for terms and conditions that limit their ability to compete in the market or expose them to undue risk. At Accenture, I worked with a Managing Director who had a philosophy which I immediately embraced and have used ever since which is "get to yes." **(You may recall I used this method with that difficult CISO in the beginning of the book.)** Get to yes really asks the negotiation team (executive sponsors, stakeholders, legal, security, data privacy) to focus on the key contractual terms and conditions that absolutely prevent the two companies from signing an agreement and looking for ways to solve through those critical areas. This means that only the "big rocks," the critical issues, are highlighted and the majority of the contractual agreement is not actually redlined because the potential redlines are not deal breakers. Additionally, where we have contractually resolved those critical issues in the past, the language that was used becomes the baseline for the new agreement unless they absolutely prevent the two companies from signing an agreement. This enables long and complex negotiations to really become short, focused negotiations to remove critical business barriers.

The interesting thing about this approach is that the issues may be the same but the resulting outcomes may be dramatically different. One time I was negotiating with a multinational technology corporation and a multinational software corporation at the same time, while also working with the same legal counsel. We were negotiating two Software as a Service (SaaS) agreements and one of the concerns was the fact that over time the cloud solution could evolve to where it was no longer a fit for the original purpose the product was purchased for. The ask of both suppliers was that we be allowed to terminate if that occurred. One company agreed to allow us to do that and incorporated our proposed language into the agreement–the second company, however, was absolutely adamant that this could not happen. They refused to allow any type of termination due to revenue recognition issues. Their response was simply: if you are afraid that will happen, then don't buy the product. Fortunately, their product actually consisted of a portfolio of integrated products so we were able to negotiate for the ability to product swap if there were products that we stopped using and additional products that we needed to use. Although we essentially had to keep the total spend amount the same, this achieved the same result through significantly different paths.

Tenet 4: Share a common communication thread with negotiation team members to share the consolidated perception of the truth. There are two sides to every story … and then there is the truth. In high executive visibility negotiations, I find it useful to identify the critical issues the team is trying to solve, the customer position, the supplier position, and the next steps to resolve the critical issues. Once that is resolved, I then work with the supplier to update the consolidated position and jointly share this with both companies' executives. This simple communication technique emphasizes the fact that we are on the same team trying to achieve positive results. It forces both parties to collectively discuss and document the key issues they are facing and their steps to resolve. This eliminates the ability for each team to "tell their side of the story to their management;" it's the same story, coauthored by both parties. There is really no room for misinterpretation since both parties wrote the status report. I normally include the current mutually agreed negotiation project plan as part of the status report to show where we are in the negotiation process and what the "big rocks" are that need to be cracked to allow us to get to yes.

One of my favorite, and most challenging negotiations, involved sourcing Enterprise Resource Planning (ERP) software services from one of the major ERP providers to support a European utility company for Accenture. Accenture was engaged in a competitive bid with multiple other Solutions Integrators (SIs) who were either offering the same ERP solution or a competitive solution. The ERP provider had partnered with multiple SIs to win the business and actually felt that our competitors were better positioned to win the business, and since they had proposed a more enhanced scope, the company would actually obtain more revenue if an alternate competitor won. We felt strongly that we were going to win the engagement and, in fact, anticipated that the client would award the business to us within the next two weeks. I received a call in Chicago on Friday and flew to Sweden over the weekend to begin negotiating with the supplier that week with a plan to come to a commercial agreement by the following Friday so that we could submit our bid to the client the next Monday.

There were several factors that added complexity to this negotiation. One, it was the suppliers quarter end and like most suppliers there were multiple other deals all vying for deal desk, legal and leadership attention. Although this was a big opportunity in Europe, globally it was not the supplier's critical priority. Two, although the ERP provider provided an integrated ERP solution, the solution that we were bidding integrated multiple cloud products that the ERP provider had acquired. The acquired companies had not been fully integrated into the parent company yet, which meant that there were separate leadership and legal teams that we would have to deal with across the globe. Three, the construct of the client agreement was an ERP as a service contract that extended over ten years. Both the service component and the contract duration presented incredible risks such as termination for convenience, product evolution and potentially even product obsolescence over the life of the agreement. This negotiation challenged my procurement skills and philosophy and ultimately forced me to refine a collaborative procurement approach that I have been using ever since and I hoped to share with you in this book.

I mention this negotiation because all of these tenets were applied. Both the supplier and my company were working collaboratively to win a deal. This required collaboration on multiple fronts. Most importantly, we had to have a price to win or the client would not select us. This meant that each company established their baseline cost and desired markup. As we consolidated the total costs to the customer, we both decided that our total cost was too high and we needed to find ways to reduce the costs through scope clarification and reduction, overall solution design, and ultimately decreased margins and contingency. Through multiple rounds of pricing negotiations and discussions, we developed a cost effective solution that was still profitable for both companies and able to meet the expected price to win. We also needed to find a way to get to yes. Tenet 4 was actually a result of this specific negotiation. That specific supplier had CEO level relationships within our company and often escalated when they were not satisfied with the progress we were making. To prevent that from happening, and also to keep track of the critical items we were negotiating, we actually created a status sheet that listed each critical topic as a row, the required client (our) ask in the first column and the current position of each of the acquired companies in the remaining columns. We color coded each company's position green, amber, or red based on the ability to meet the client requirement. Using this color coding, we were able to present a dashboard view of the entire negotiation across each of the products that was shared with both project teams and with our respective executive leadership teams. Additionally, by presenting the independent views of each of the companies, as well as how we were able to get to yes for a specific company, we were able to share best practices and creative solutions across those different organizations and find multiple ways to get to yes. Ultimately, we were able to come to high level terms across our respective five companies by the end of the week to present our proposal to the client that following Monday. It is amazing what can happen when you take a collaborative Win-Win-Win approach to a negotiation. Next we'll go over an additional tip, a concept that I have found very helpful for negotiation.

Push Until They Say No

When you're in negotiations with a vendor, you want to ask them until they say no. My premise has always been that the way sales teams are structured, and the overall revenue of the deal—I'm empowered to approve certain deals. Once the revenue goes too low, I have to elevate it to my VP or Senior VP. In some cases it goes too low for them and it has to go to the CRO, or the CFO. That doesn't mean it isn't a profitable deal for the company, but the acceptable margins are low enough it involves a significant discussion with executive leadership. The same applies for the vendors during a negotiation. When I'm negotiating a deal, I try to negotiate directly with their CRO and the CFO, because in the grand scheme of things, they have the final say. If I'm talking to the sales team and they aren't involving their CFO or Senior VP, in my mind we haven't hit a market competitive price. I want to get to the point where the vendor says, "This is my final and best offer." Then I know I'm achieving my best price in the market. No disrespect to sales teams, but my goal is to be negotiating with the Senior VP, or CFO, because they are the ultimate decision maker.

Now that you have a good understanding of the value of collaboration during a negotiation, let's take a closer look at what each side wants during a negotiation.

Chapter 5
A Win for the Business

My first procurement experience was with IBM, it was sales, but I was working on a major $2 billion dollar telecommunications outsourcing contract. I was working in what we called the Contract Control Request (CCR) team. Basically, if the customer needed a new product or service they would come to us and say we need this. We would work with the team to put together a proposal, present it to the customer, and the customer would review it and send edits back. We'd negotiate the proposal, provide pricing, and sometimes it would get accepted, sometimes not. Then we would sign the document and implement the change. When I first joined, the changes were averaging thirty days or more to complete a change. It could be everything from a $10K request to a $250K request, but it was taking up the full thirty days. What I had to do was draft a letter that explained the scope of the changes and then I handed that to my legal team who ripped it to shreds, re-edited my language and returned a "tomato soup" document full of red lines. Then I had to go through pricing, which took a couple weeks to get approved. I was never sure if the customer would accept the pricing or not. What I learned was that the speed and efficiency wasn't there at all.

After my first somewhat traumatic experience, I worked with legal to create two CCR templates, a fixed price template and a time and materials template. Using those templates, I could simply fill out the template with minimal if any red lines. From a pricing standpoint, I went to financing and we agreed to apply our pre-negotiated rate card that listed the cost per resource type. If I used the pre-negotiated rate card,

I didn't have to seek approval from finance. I also convinced the customer to agree to approve a high level statement of work with rough order of magnitude pricing *prior* to actual creation of a detailed agreement. That meant I could go to the customer and say, "We've looked at this request and created our high level statement of work. Based on your request, it's going to cost $250K. Do you agree to approve this change if the price is $250K plus or minus 10 percent." If they agreed, I would work with the team to create and submit a detailed contract to the customer. Due to these simple changes, we could get critical deals negotiated and signed in a day. We took our overall process time from thirty days down to one week for standard contracts and one day for critical ones.

Unfortunately, in many companies, from a business standpoint, procurement is often perceived as a blocking organization instead of a trusted advisor. That perception spawns from challenging engagements with procurement that resulted in a less than satisfied customer. If I break down the root cause of dissatisfaction, these are some of the common themes:

1. procurement took too long or did not meet my timeline
2. the procurement process was very cumbersome
3. procurement did not understand my requirements
4. procurement was only focused on savings
5. procurement did not keep me informed on the status of my project

The overarching theme of each of these is a disconnection between the process the stakeholder expected to experience and the process the stakeholder actually experienced. One thing that will assist with increasing stakeholder satisfaction is level setting stakeholder expectations. One of the common questions I am asked is how long will a project take. As a former consultant, I rely on my standard answer for everything... "it depends" but in this case, "it depends" is in fact an incredibly accurate statement. If you think about the end-to-end procurement process and all of the things that happen, the answer to the question is based on a multitude of items that are completely outside of procurement control.

Let's look at the process at a high level to explain further. Assuming a complex competitive bid scenario, the key steps from identifying the procurement need to receiving the actual product or services would be to:

- Define the project requirements
- Identify potential bidders
- Complete the NDA
- Define the RFP requirements
- Submit the RFP
- Answer bidder questions
- Develop scorecard
- Receive responses
- Evaluate vendors
- Select vendors for demonstration
- Complete demonstrations
- Evaluate vendors and downselect for proof of concept
- Complete proof of concept
- Evaluate vendors and downselect final vendor(s)
- Complete security assessment
- Complete reference checks
- Negotiate contract
- Negotiate Data Protection Amendment (DPA)
- Negotiate security assessment (VRA)
- Negotiate SLAs
- Finalize commercial negotiations
- Set up vendor in the accounts payable system
- Obtain purchase approvals

- Sign contract
- Issue PO
- Receive product or service
- Pay suppliers

As you can see from the long list of process steps, procurement is not responsible for or even accountable for these steps; however, to complete the end-to-end process and ultimately receive the product or service, these process steps must be completed. Business stakeholders prefer a "single hand to shake" versus having to engage all the entities in the end-to-end process. Procurement acts as the overall project manager and manages through the end-to-end process on behalf of the stakeholder. A handy tool that I have used to successfully explain this process to my stakeholders is a "Procurement Process on a Page Diagram" that outlines the process flow and provides high level timelines for simple, medium complexity and high complexity projects. That timeline needs to include the kickoff points for key subprocess steps such as kicking off a Vendor Risk Assessment, DPA review or supplier setup request.

Developing the "Procurement Process on a Page" and sharing that proactively with your stakeholders will assist in level setting their expectations and understanding the complexity of the end-to-end process. Another question that often arises is: "When do I need to engage procurement?" I have always answered that question with: "As soon as you identify the need to buy something." I use that answer because I always prefer to be engaged earlier in the process than later.

When I am engaged earlier in the process, then I can follow a standard process. I had a CIO engage me to discuss a project that he had negotiated with me. He had essentially completed the negotiation and was ready to sign it. He just wanted me to check it over. His expectation was that the contract would be reviewed and he could sign it that day.

When I reviewed the agreement, I immediately asked him to stop negotiating with the supplier and refer them directly to me!

He was looking to procure a Big Data Services provider which at the time was an emerging industry. The supplier had proposed and he had agreed to a multi-year, committed spend agreement with them. His assumption was that the business functions would use the product and be so enamored by the product that they would definitely meet the spend commitment. The agreement started at less than $1 million in year one then dramatically scaled to upwards of $10 million.

A quick analysis of the pilot projects the supplier had completed indicated that only a small percentage of the users intended to continue to use the supplier, and other business unit CIOs had clearly expressed that they did not want to allocate any budget to supporting this supplier. Additionally, from a market price benchmarking exercise, they were incredibly expensive.

I was able to renegotiate the agreement and move from a committed spend agreement to a consumption-based agreement and created a rate card or a low, medium and high complexity sprint that enabled the business to easily select and pay for exactly what they needed. In the first three years, the total consumed spend had risen to approximately $3 million; however, that was $5 million less than what the committed spend agreement had contemplated and would have committed for.

Although I was able to obtain a successful negotiation outcome, I was engaged incredibly late in the process versus when the need to purchase the product was first identified. When engaged at the right time frame, procurement has the ability to work with the stakeholders to define the competitive landscape and, if possible, set the stage for a competitive bidding opportunity.

Engaging procurement early in the buying process and following the procurement process enables the team to obtain the best information to make the right decision from a supplier selection standpoint. Early engagement facilitates developing an understanding of the competitive landscape, creates the ability to identify multiple potential suppliers and sets the stage for a competitive bid. Whenever possible, and especially for high spend projects, I really prefer to competitively bid multiple suppliers to achieve a successful procurement negotiation. The competitive bid approach really provides the team with the information needed to make an informed decision, including the ability to compare and contrast multiple solutions, understand different supplier approaches, compare solution scope and pricing, negotiate for market competitive pricing and negotiate for critical contractual requirements. Level setting stakeholder expectations using the Procurement Process on a Page will help resolve the challenges associated with the timeline and overall complexity of the end-to end process.

Regarding understanding stakeholder requirements, stakeholder engagement is critical to the successful completion of the project. One of my favorite sayings is: "If someone says they are an expert in IT, then they are a liar or an idiot." I am not trying to be crass in that comment, what I am really trying to say is that the complexity of IT is unparalleled, and no one is able to become an expert in all things IT. I rely on my stakeholders and their expertise in their specific job functions to help define the suppliers that they want to consider in an upcoming procurement project. In most cases, the key stakeholders in any global company have often worked with a plethora of suppliers in their current and past employers and will have a good understanding of the market. When they do not, then obviously there are plenty of supplier evaluation tools out there that can be leveraged such as Forrester, Gartner, International Data Corporation (IDC), etc.

Meeting In The Middle Isn't Always A Win

When negotiating with suppliers to meet stakeholder requirements, one trap that procurement teams sometimes fall into is assuming that meeting in the middle is good. That is not always the case. Case in point, when working for an IT outsourcing company we were being pushed by our client to accept extended payment terms and as a result, subsequently attempted to flow down those requests to the suppliers. For example, clients began to ask for 60-day payment terms. Our standard supplier agreements were 30-day payment terms. We, therefore, asked our suppliers to move to 60-day payment terms as well. The supplier subsequently proposed 45-day payment terms and my team wanted to accept the compromise. Unfortunately, that compromise was not acceptable, because this was a case where meeting in the middle wasn't a win. Moving to 45-day payment terms would mean that we would have to pay our supplier before we were paid by the customer and would have created a negative cash flow situation. Based on that, the team realized why this was so critical and worked diligently to explain why the extended term was such a critical requirement for the business and were able to get suppliers to extend the payment terms further than normal.

Stoplight Chart

Documenting the critical stakeholder requirements and using that as a stoplight chart is an effective tool to ensure that stakeholder requirements are clearly understood and met throughout the negotiation. I ensure that the issues are captured on the status chart and are moved from red to yellow when a commercial or contractual resolution has been proposed and then moved from Yellow to Green when the appropriate language has been accepted in the contractual agreement. This ensures that all requirements are captured and all requirements are met.

Although a savings calculation will be created at the end from a procurement reporting standpoint, that is not the overall focus of the negotiation. When we do report savings, we do not report the savings as a procurement savings only but instead report it as savings resulting from collaboration with the business, legal, risk, security and procurement. The end-to-end process cannot be completed without all of these agencies involved.

The last item to manage from a stakeholder perspective is to ensure that stakeholders are informed of the project status at all times. This can be a challenge especially in high volume environments where sourcing resources are managing 15-25 simultaneous projects. I have developed and implemented multiple communication mechanisms to keep stakeholders informed. For very complex negotiations similar to my global ERP example, we essentially had one slide, the stoplight chart, because that was a very compressed negotiation. For "normal projects," I use a high level mutually-agreed-to project milestone chart that consists of key deliverables and dates that are required from the extended project team in addition to the stoplight chart.

I have a project template that includes the team, negotiation plan, pricing analysis sheet and contract summary sheet that is used to conduct complex negotiations only and can be used to generate all required project updates and communications. I prefer to keep the communication requirements as simple and easy to manage as possible to support high volumes of sourcing projects and maintain stakeholder alignment.

Conceptually, I have discussed collaboration with our stakeholders to level set expectations, understand requirements, meet those requirements and manage communications. Now let's talk about the basic requirements and how procurement needs to evolve to manage the new demands of digital metamorphosis!

As discussed before, the digital metamorphosis has created multiple options for companies to buy, build, and buy or design and build their own software solution. The acceleration of technology coupled with the current talent challenge means that, for a stakeholder, the requirements that they are procuring today may undergo significant changes over the next one to three years. This is critical to not just defining the term of the agreement but also understanding the variability in the industry and how to mitigate the risk of change when you negotiate the vendor agreements. A list of key things to consider when evaluating the risk of change are:

1. Are requirements known or shifting?
2. Is the pace of technology changing rapidly or slowly?
3. Are regulations and legislation static or constantly evolving?
4. Is the product or service mature or emerging?
5. Is the product an integrated part of an ecosystem or a stand-alone product?
6. Is the technology flexible or is it proprietary and rigid?
7. How quickly can the business bring the product to market?
8. Is the desired relationship a true strategic partnership or a simple supplier relationship?

"Procurement played a critical role in driving business performance and cost savings in a decentralized multinational organization. They first convinced the supplier to switch from a market-centric to a global service model, and then collaborated with corporate and business unit teams to evolve strategy and processes to support this new service model." –FeiFei H, Head of Digital Channel Innovation

Chapter 6
A Win for the Supplier

"When Eric explained his Win-Win-Win approach, procurement went from being a sales prohibiting roadblock to an invaluable partner and even a silver bullet." –Laura R., Google Sales Executive

One of the reasons why I decided to write this book is that many of the suppliers I have worked with told me that I had a unique approach to procurement. A sales executive from Google, Laura R., summed it up for me when she said, "In most large enterprise companies procurement is a team to avoid like the plague as often they will slow down the sales process and add red tape. When a procurement team is built with a strategic leader who understands the company's business needs and has the ear of executive leadership then working with the procurement team can be an invaluable partner and even a silver bullet."

Jennifer Dominguez, a Growth Advisor for eSellas who previously worked in supply chain and procurement with me, sent me this about her experience from both sides of a negotiation:

"Why did I make a career move to supply chain/procurement? I was lucky to have a long career with one company, or actually a series of companies that evolved through mergers and acquisitions. I led sales enablement teams and held several roles in account management. I had a perspective on contracts we negotiated with our clients, and I was an internal customer to procurement as we leveraged a variety of suppliers to provide services to our end clients. So when I had the chance to move into procurement, I looked forward to having an opportunity to sit on the other side of the table as a buyer.

"I led a team of talented procurement professionals handling the technology category, and enjoyed learning the ins and outs of strategic sourcing. I gained a whole new perspective on what makes a good supplier. Our 'best' partners:

- *Were deliberate about understanding our business*
- *Communicated well, were highly collaborative, and could clearly articulate the value they provided*
- *Demonstrated creativity in solving problems*
- *Added value beyond the core scope; for example, leveraging other expertise or providing advice*

"I have since moved back into a sales role, and have taken those lessons with me, striving to be the kind of supplier and partner that I was looking for through the procurement lens.

"How did I perceive the value of strategic sourcing from a sales perspective?

"As the leader of a strategic sales function, sourcing was a critical ingredient in our win strategy through two main channels:

1. *The pillars of our solution often had components that were not part of our capability set and had to be sourced through other companies. We typically were working under tight deadlines to turn around a proposal and had to work with partners who could respond with commitments and pricing very quickly. Our most effective partners had representatives who were dedicated to our team, knew our business, and knew how to integrate quickly with solutions and a proposed approach, appearing as a seamless part of the extended enterprise. The very best partners brought added value to the table; client relationships they were willing to leverage, investment funds or pilot programs they were willing to access, and thought leadership to*

share. Those partners were the most frequently utilized, based on their ability to help us differentiate and win.

2. *As a large technology company, we had significant purchasing power with technology suppliers that often surpassed discounts our clients were able to secure on their own. As part of our pursuits, we analyzed the client's technology spend, even for areas outside of the scope of the deal, to identify additional savings we could broker on their behalf. This became part of the 'total cost of ownership' view of the deal, adding to the overall bottom line financial benefit and providing additional value to our clients."*

If you recall, earlier in the book I mentioned my goal from a procurement standpoint. If you put yourself in your suppliers' shoes, you can see that they actually have a very similar goal to procurement; their key objectives are to align with their stakeholders, understand their priorities, ensure that their goods and services have the ability to align and meet the needs of the stakeholders, set their expectations and drive a successful business relationship via long term relationships, volume growth, product growth and collaboration. As procurement, we're trying to find the right supplier, and the supplier is trying to convince the stakeholder/purchaser that they are the right supplier. That's the only difference. So our job boils down to providing the stakeholder the right information so they can make the correct decision on the supplier. Oftentimes, we neglect to think of the bigger picture and miss out on opportunities to create stronger global relationships between our stakeholders and suppliers.

For instance, if you think about global technology companies, there are many that sell large portfolios of products. When I consider my former SI employers, they had a slightly different perspective on cloud solutions providers. Some cloud solution integrators didn't care which cloud supplier the client picked–it could be any of the big three–most of the SI's were "cloud agnostic" (although there may be a preference for a specific technology).

One SI was different from the other companies because they had a preferred cloud supplier and because of that, they had a very strong relationship with that provider. In fact, the relationship was so strong, they considered this SI company a strategic global customer.

Interestingly, I've worked at other companies that actually had more global spend with that same provider but were not treated as a global strategic customer. In these instances, we didn't have a global account lead or a very strategic relationship with them; they basically managed our relationship at a product level, instead of at an overall company level relationship.

At one company, for instance, I wanted to establish a strategic global relationship with our cloud provider, so I worked across each of their product lines to establish one. Step one, the supplier created a global account lead. Step two, I worked with the product leads to review product-by-product and renegotiated the agreements to put the best possible agreements in place between us. We established multiple global agreements, moved some of our resellers to preferred resellers, and greatly expanded our relationship across all the product lines. The prices went down; as a result, we were able to buy more, and we established a much more strategic relationship.

Another example of a win for the supplier was with a CRM (Customer Relationship Management) technology company. We had established multiple country specific agreements, which meant we were paying different pricing in different regions and countries, across the board, which made no sense. We negotiated to put a single global agreement in place with standardized pricing for all the markets. Obviously it was a price reduction, and when you reduce the pricing, there's a revenue impact to the supplier because they lose revenue when they lower their prices. But because they were willing to lower their prices, we were able to bring in other business units and different countries, which increased their overall spend, while decreasing the unit price. This reduction in cost enabled us to open up more international markets, and today they are in over thirty countries because of our strong global relationship with them.

Selling A Field Of Dreams

If you have ever seen the movie *Field of Dreams* starring Kevin Costner, you will probably remember the image of Ray creating the baseball field in the middle of the cornfield so that the ghosts of the baseball legends would show up to play ball. Now that we understand the concept of the Win-Win-Win strategy, let's talk about defining what a field of dreams looks like for all parties and convincing your stakeholders and suppliers to build the field with you.

The Win-Win-Win strategy is trying to find a win for everyone. Ideally, the business is going to win, the supplier is going to sell more units, and that will get funneled through procurement, because the more we buy, the lower the price becomes.

The field of dreams is slightly different, it pertains to what happens when we have to buy when we can't make a commitment. Most companies, when they're selling products to another company, will come to you and say, for instance, "How many employees do you have? I'm going to base my pricing on how many licenses you're going to need."

The challenge we run into is that there are times we don't know the answer to that question, and we have to say, "I don't know." Obviously, the price goes down the more we buy, but sometimes we don't know the exact information the company is looking for.

Often, this happened to me when I was acting as a Solution Integrator negotiating third-party agreements to develop a market offering, or as a procurement representative negotiating a solution that would be offered to independent insurance agents or franchisees. I was able to negotiate on behalf of a stakeholder who was attempting to offer a solution to their end customers. This meant there was an intent to purchase but no ability to commit to that purchase. This required an understanding of every available negotiation lever that could be pulled to offer the best possible solution to the end customer and finding a way to navigate both business and the supplier's ability to pull those levers. Some of the key levers to consider were term, volume, scope, pricing and market characteristics.

From a term standpoint, I prefer to negotiate a three-year agreement in a stable market and a one-year agreement in either an emerging market or a market where there are rapidly occurring changes (such as the mobile phone market). If you are confident that the supplier solution will remain viable for the full three years; sure that there are no emerging technologies, regulations or new entries into the market, a longer team agreement is a great option. Alternatively, if there is no ability to transition suppliers in less than one to two years; then negotiating a three-year agreement enables both procurement and the supplier to leverage three times the potential spend of a one-year agreement and, ideally, enables a reduction in the required supplier margin. This creates a more attractive price and also reinforces the desire to create a long-term strategic relationship. Three-year deals can also be extended further with additional renewal options beyond the initial term. Ideally, if the relationship is progressing well and there are no significant market condition changes, then the agreement can simply be extended. In cases where the supplier relationship is less than optimal, there are dramatic market or legislative changes that could impact the solution, or multiple commodity suppliers in a price competitive market, then a one or two-year agreement may be the preferred option.

The volume of products and the scope of products are another key factor to consider. Since the field of dreams concept is a non-committed spend agreement, the focus is on negotiating volume-based pricing tiers that are realized over time as the relationship between all parties grows vs. negotiating for the lowest possible price immediately. By creating pricing tiers based on the expected sales volume anticipated over the life of the agreement, each entity desires to reach that highest tier. There are several things to consider when creating tiered pricing. First and foremost, do not punish the early adopters. Tiered pricing should reduce the price for all purchasers of the product. This is relatively easy for software customers as the cost to purchase or maintain software products can simply be reduced over time as the number of licensed users increases. This is a little more complicated for hardware products where the initial purchases are sunk costs for the early adopters and follow-on purchasers are able to achieve the volume incentives. This can be offset through the use of credits. Many OEMs receive credits or price concessions from their component manufacturers based on the size of the order. These credits can ultimately be flowed through to their customers. Another option is to discount non-hardware based components of the end-to-end solution, e.g. maintenance or support charges based on achievement of specific volume tiers.

A second thing to consider is making the tiers attractive to all regions. Any multinational corporation today will have entities in developing countries, emerging markets, developed countries and many countries in between. It is incredibly difficult to establish tiered pricing that is competitive in India and profitable in the US. There is often no one-size-fits-all pricing solution, so if that is the case, acknowledge that fact and establish tiered pricing based on geographic regions, market sizes, market pricing or any other factor that gives both procurement and the supplier the opportunity to create market competitive pricing globally.

In this particular example, I worked with a supplier to create and implement a tiered pricing based on overall market size that provided discounts globally as the relationship expanded. We rapidly ran into two challenges; one the pricing in the US was not being sufficiently impacted as the overall relationship increased; and two, the pricing in many of the emerging markets was not as cost competitive as their competitor's pricing. We were able to go back to the drawing board and restructure how the different market tiers were defined and also able to improve the overall discounts in the US market so that as the global volume increased the US pricing decreased. Although we did not get the pricing right the first time, we collaboratively renegotiated a better price that made the solution more attractive globally and allowed us to expand faster than we thought possible; so fast, in fact, that in addition to a negotiation to solve the two aforementioned challenges, we also had to add additional tiers to our pricing volume!

In addition to setting tiered based pricing, look for opportunities to grow the suite of supplier products that you use. Although we initially consolidated our spend on one supplier, we identified another supplier, who had a better technical solution and who offered a more enhanced scope of products that enabled us to replace both the original supplier as well as other suppliers who had complementary products.

We had similar success using another testing supplier. Initially one US business unit was interested in using the supplier. This supplier provided a platform fee and a volume based fee. During our initial negotiations, the initial business unit was incredibly confident that other business units in the US and abroad would want to adopt that solution. They intentionally ordered more volume than they needed at the time so they could pool the cost with those other business units. Their prediction was soon validated as multiple other US and international business units joined the agreement. By sharing the platform and allocating the costs, they were able to dramatically reduce their cost and increase the supplier spend tenfold, resulting in another negotiation to increase the tier volumes. They essentially created a robust technology solution that was adopted by other markets as their eCommerce presence matured to the point of requiring these services.

In short, I have applied the Win-Win-Win strategy and the field of dreams methodology across hundreds of negotiations with multiple suppliers. Many suppliers have adopted and applied that approach with amazing results! I even had one supplier respond to a proposal with the tagline: *"Custom proposal based on 'Field of Dreams' vision alignment with key stakeholders."*

In summary, the key things to consider when building your own field of dreams with your suppliers are listed below:

Develop the Win-Win-Win Strategy to grow together

Align expectations with vendors (field of dreams mentality)

Focus on the customer and the customer's customer

Help the customer drive growth and meet their strategic business objectives

Apply tiered pricing and flexible terms for mutually beneficial growth

Reduce costs and make offerings competitive in the smaller markets and GEOs

Unfortunately, we do not always get it right. In cases where we miss, we take the time to approach the supplier and determine why we are not growing strategically and what steps we need to take to correct it. As mentioned above, they are typically due to pricing misses where the pricing is not competitive or can also be based on contractual terms and conditions that make it too risky for the business. I have also had cases where suppliers have contradicted the 'field of dreams' mentality through actions such as demanding price increases in conjunction with volume increases or threatening to shut off licenses if a renewal dead-line was missed. In those cases, suppliers who are "penny wise and pound foolish" will be able to capture a short-term gain but will typically negotiate themselves out of a long-term strategic relationship.

Now that we've examined the negotiation from the supplier side, in the next chapter we'll be covering an issue that causes many procurement organizations to fail—not being fast enough.

Chapter 7
Are You Built to Run
At Digital Speed?

"I want to make procurement invisible to my stakeholders." -Reunan Varene

What a profound statement, "I want to make procurement invisible to my stakeholders" especially coming from someone who, like me, had worked in procurement outsourcing and who had focused so much on stakeholder collaboration. But that is exactly what Reunan Varene told me when I met him shortly after he had taken over as the CPO of Dropbox.

Both Reunan and I had realized that for the majority of the stakeholder purchases, especially those where we already have pre-existing agreements in place with our suppliers, the goal should be that the business can easily find and buy the products and services they need every day. In an ideal world, once the architecture team defines the standard, procurement or a procurement representative should contract with the vendor and then provide a procurement process and tool to facilitate the buying process. I have attempted multiple times to create that capability, however, I personally have not seen an effective commercial procurement tool out there that truly meets the need. These are the things that I have tried to work on and where I have and have not been successful.

First, I have tried to implement some type of governance to manage technology supplier purchases. As previously discussed, the pace that technology is growing is unprecedented. New technologies come to life and cease to be relevant every day. Additionally, many companies offer free versions and downloadable access to their products. Couple that with a transitory workforce who become accustomed to using different products at their prior employers and you have an unprecedented demand for a diverse set of technology products. This raises challenges from a governance, support, security, procurement and legal standpoint as more and more supplier requests are created. Technology governance is important to manage the flow of requests. Simply having approved standards and veto rights will reduce the number of requests that need to be processed. Although no one likes to tell a stakeholder no, companies cannot manage multiple redundant technologies due to stakeholder preference. Please note that I do not consider technology governance to be part of the procurement process; however, the approval of a procurement request by technology governance is critical to the success of technology procurement.

Once a request is approved, procurement and, more specifically, the contracting process kicks in. Sometimes this can be the fastest or longest part of the process and that normally boils down to risk and price. Risk is critical in today's technology world. We have all seen the news headlines reporting the latest data breach. Companies and products are under attack and there are huge repercussions associated with data breaches. It can take as much time to negotiate (and in some cases may not even be possible to negotiate) a high-risk, low spend contract as a high risk, high spend contract. With the increased demand and limited resources, risk based contracting is a method of defining the contracting process based on the level of risk.

First, a set of questions are developed to define the risk associated with the product or service. The set traditionally consists of questions such as: Are you accessing Personally Identifiable Information (PII), credit card data, etc., or are you accessing production data? The answer to these questions will determine if the product or service is considered to be high-, medium- or low-risk. Any suppliers that score high will require a negotiated agreement using the company's or supplier's standard contract template. If the answer is medium or low and the spend is below a set spend threshold (e.g. under $50K), then an accelerated contracting path may be used. In the accelerated contracting path, the supplier agreement is reviewed (using the get to yes philosophy) to minimize or eliminate any required negotiations. Companies with sophisticated automation teams can sometimes automate the process of reading through the contract to identify deviations to their standard preferred language so that legal can review the summary results vs. the entire agreement. If the vendor agreement is deemed to be acceptable, then the agreement is simply signed with no legal negotiations. If some deviations exist, a risk acceptance letter may be generated by legal for the stakeholder that must be accepted before signature. Where major deviations exist, the stakeholder may be asked to seek an alternate provider or procurement and legal may negotiate an agreement using the company's or supplier's standard contract template.

There are also opportunities to work with cloud marketplaces such as Amazon Web Services (AWS or resellers such as Insight) and actually leverage the contract template that they negotiate with their suppliers. AWS has created their own template to contract business through the marketplace. If the company can review and agree to adopt that AWS agreement in lieu of their standard agreement then essentially the AWS agreement and the signed acceptance form govern the relationship instead of a company specific legal agreement. This enables the company to use AWS to focus on the less critical supplier deals available through the marketplace and the company to focus on specific critical deals.

When procurement does negotiate the contract, the end result is that the contract and the pricing information should be input into the procurement tool and clearly cataloged so that it can be presented to corporate employees if they want to purchase that product or service.

Today, that is one of the biggest challenges I have seen in the procurement space. First, historically, pricing is not normally included in master agreements. Many companies follow the philosophy of an evergreen master agreement that does not include pricing and add the pricing in the purchasing agreements. What ends up happening is a complex and confusing series of contracts that are challenging to manage and understand. Second, evergreen agreements do not expire while the pace of data privacy, security and legal requirements do. Think about the changes required due to GDPR for example and the pace is only accelerating! Additionally, as people are promoted, retire or leave the company, the contractual experience ends up being lost. Few companies have the resources to dedicate to input contractual information into the procurement database, much less manage complex legacy agreements. I prefer a three-year master agreement with embedded global tiered volume pricing and defined renewal options as a much cleaner contracting approach.

Including the spend in the contractual agreement enables the pricing to be cataloged into the procurement tool once under the correct commodity code and spend category so that the information is captured correctly and not improperly based on multitude miscategorized purchase orders. I would love to say that the spend data I have seen across any of the multiple companies I worked for was accurate, however, that was and probably still is an incredible challenge.

Corporate Amazon

Recently I went to a scope conference and I noticed multiple companies that were selling band analytics solutions to help procurement analyze their spend. The reason they're doing that is because our procurement tools are incredibly complicated and convoluted. In many cases, the people who are buying goods and services are categorizing it the wrong way. A good example is Amazon, they could be categorized as cloud infrastructure, but someone may call it a bookseller. It could happen!

Another problem is that after a merger or acquisition, companies often end up with multiple systems that are too expensive or complex to integrate. These outdated tools don't allow us to analyze our spend correctly, and vendors are noticing this gap in the market and trying to provide a solution. The direction I see the industry heading in is automated, user-friendly, and for lack of a better word, Amazon-like.

There are two major challenges in our industry I have attempted to address that I have not been able to overcome (yet). One, I have attempted to work with multiple automation teams to reformat the procurement contract template into an "automation-friendly" version that could easily be imported into a procurement tool by an automated bot. I have not been able to accomplish that yet, however as AI and automation progress, I think that will be a quick win.

The other thing that I would love to see, but have not been able to complete yet is the concept of a "Corporate Amazon." I've talked to multiple procurement to payment providers about their system capabilities and from a procurement tool standpoint, Amazon is the benchmark! I assume that most, if not all of you, have used Amazon for your personal shopping needs. Think about how seamless that User Interface (UI) and User Experience (UX) are. You log in, search for an item via the search bar or by browsing categories, you see multiple available items, select the item you want, select the best price, add it to your cart and buy it! Nothing could be more simple … now think about your procurement tool.

For the power user, it's probably a similar experience; they can very easily do the same thing. But think about the concept of a power user … why do you even need one? It's probably because a "casual user" cannot figure out the complexity of the procurement tool on their own and gets too frustrated trying to use it. What is the value of having a tool that requires specialized resources to buy things for your employees?

There is also a concern that if employees were empowered and able to buy things, they would go out and buy things on their own that they should not and we would not be able to control our spending. The reality is that this often happens today anyway, that is why there are audit teams auditing expense reports to find software purchases and technology purchases that were not made through the approved cumbersome, complex and time-consuming process. The solution is simple in theory and hopefully soon in technology.

We should create an "Amazon-like" corporate procurement tool. In today's world, team members often have to go to a tool such as Service Now to request a laptop, a travel tool such as Concur to request travel and a procurement tool to order a screen protector for their new laptop. What if we just create a single procurement tool, e.g. "Shop Now" as the single front door to access all of these systems and when a team member requests a laptop, flight reservation, or privacy screen, they are routed to the appropriate fulfillment channel? This simplifies the user experience and they now only need to remember one place to go.

From a procurement tool standpoint, the "Corporate Amazon" should only offer the products and services that are approved by governance and the corporation to buy. Those lists of items should consist of miscellaneous products and services available through a marketplace (think Amazon or Ebay for business), cloud services providers' marketplaces (think AWS or Google marketplace) distributor or value added reseller agreements and direct agreements with OEMs. These products have all been vetted and approved by the business for use and are searchable to find and add to your cart. Ideally, they are searchable by keyword (e.g. CRM Software or direct search e.g. Braze). If a team member searches for a product that is not available in "Corporate Amazon" then they would need to fill out a request that would go through the architecture approval and once approved route to procurement to negotiate the agreement through the risk-based contracting, cloud marketplace, value added reseller or direct negotiation process. This is essentially the only time that the stakeholder would actually need to engage procurement and procurement would predominantly focus on critical supplier negotiations and major product renewals.

Having a simplified procurement tool will significantly increase your ability to control spend under management via your procurement tool versus via autocratic procurement policies! One of the critical things to consider is the overall approval process. The end-to-end procurement process is lengthy to begin with. You start with competitive bidding, demonstrations, proofs of concept, commercial negotiations, contract negotiations, security and data privacy negotiations and those are required to get to the point where the stakeholder can make a purchase. I have worked with companies that had divisions that required two steps in their approval process (business manager and finance) and divisions that required over fifteen approvals (multiple business managers and multiple finance approvers). In those processes, the majority of the fifteen approvers were so far removed from the actual purchasing decision that they were simply a rubber stamp and had no idea what was even being approved. In some cases, especially in Q4, those approvers were frequently removed from the process because they were on holiday and we were trying to close a critical end of quarter or end of year deal.

Having incredibly onerous procurement processes ultimately does not benefit anyone. This is especially evident in the IT outsourcing industry as many purchases are actually required to support customer deals. The more onerous and difficult the process, the more lengthy the process to procure the products and, ultimately, the slower the ability to generate revenue. The other thing to consider is the reaction time needed to respond to technology innovation and security threats.

Collaboration with architecture approvers, the business and finance approvers, and the respective parties, in the end-to-end procurement process are critical to ensure you have the most efficient and effective procurement and approval processes to move at digital speed!

Chapter 8
Building a Digital Procurement Organization

"We didn't focus on being the first phone call when our stakeholders needed something, we focused on calling them. Once we established that relationship, they engaged us earlier when we had more influence." -Brittany K., CPO

"What has been your most successful accomplishment in procurement so far?" I asked Erin, a woman who was interviewing for a position on my team. I expected to hear her explain an amazing sourcing project and the tremendous savings she had managed to achieve … instead she gave me an answer that made me want to hire her on the spot. She said, "I was super excited when I was able to build a strong relationship with my stakeholders."

What an amazing answer! I knew she was a perfect fit, because she was already employing the Win-Win-Win strategy, without even knowing it.

Another person I interviewed for my team was a woman named Mona, an Executive Assistant who was interested in doing something different and joining procurement. Mona had amazing people skills, but no procurement experience. One of the first tasks I assigned Mona was to help our stakeholders build a new test lab. I specifically asked her to request free or heavily discounted products from the equipment vendors which was a task that initially made her uncomfortable. The reality and perspective that I was able to impress upon her is that for a vendor, the opportunity to have equipment in a demonstration test lab that would be viewed by hundreds or even thousands of potential customers was way more than the discounted price of the equipment. Once she felt comfortable with that, she was able to engage with multiple vendors and drive almost half a million dollars in savings. Although she initially did not have the procurement skills, she had the people management and relationship skills to convince vendors to support our test lab vision!

I have designed and built multiple global procurement organizations designed to manage the IT category or all categories of spend. The primary focus for all of those organizations has been engagement with stakeholders first and foremost. By hiring team members with the right skills to engage with the business stakeholders, build and establish relationships with them and ultimately develop procurement project pipelines, we have been able to successfully hit our savings targets.

In addition to stakeholder relationships, there is obviously a need for sourcing skills. One of the questions I always ask an employer is: Can I hire my own team? The answer is always yes. I then ask if I can hire the best people I can find. Again, the answer is yes. And the last and loaded question is: Do they have to be local or can they be anywhere? This is usually where there is a pause and the interviewer says, "We really prefer local resources." The challenge is that you can't hire the best talent in the world in one city, even a city as big as Chicago or Dallas. Another challenge is that you cannot support global procurement requirements from one country; global procurement organizations will typically require teams in all major regions (US, LATAM, EMEA, Asia, and India). The last challenge is that you cannot effectively staff a large global procurement organization cost effectively using on-shore resources only. For most companies, we empowered procurement organizations across the globe with the ability to negotiate a global agreement. That way, whichever country had the imminent and immediate need was empowered to negotiate a global deal. This also enabled us to leverage a global workforce with the ability to flex resources from one region to the other. This meant that the US was the primary region to support the US and Canada; however, they were supported by an offshore team in India and nearshore teams in LATAM to complete any global or US specific deal in that region.

In short, I only hire people who already practice the Win-Win-Win strategy. And when I'm building a strategic team, I'm thinking on a global scale, and structuring it for engagement.

Hiring a team is one thing, but developing those resources into an amazing procurement team is another. I see many companies who have strategic sourcing and procurement and to me that has never made sense. If I think about a desired career path from buyer to sourcing to strategic sourcing and ultimately to Director and CPO, having a clearly defined career path is beneficial. Additionally, when I think about relationships with strategic partners, there are requirements to negotiate enterprise agreements, and there are also requirements to negotiate purchase orders. Instead of having two organizations negotiating with the same vendors, I created pods of people with strategic sourcing, sourcing and buyers to negotiate with the same vendor for different use cases. The strategic sourcing managers are responsible for mentoring and growing their respective teams.

Our overall team focus has been stakeholder engagement. In large procurement organizations, we normally had technology category leads assigned to each major business unit to meet with key stakeholders, define the procurement opportunity log and to support execution of procurement projects by the category specific sourcing teams. In smaller organizations, I actually assigned each procurement resource specific stakeholders to manage, because building those ongoing relationships facilitates early engagement. Since each resource may not have the specific category knowledge, we collaborate as a team to share knowledge across the group. If you have ten resources with ten years experience who don't collaborate, your team only has ten years of knowledge. If they collaboratively discuss lessons learned and best practices, you can have 100 years of knowledge. We call that collaboration developing "tribal knowledge." As Larry Fox, a colleague of mine and former Global Technology Director at Accenture who has worked with me across multiple organizations puts it, "Actively practicing tribal knowledge learning concepts, constantly sharing and learning from your team, enables your procurement team to gain and maintain leadership positions."

Larry's (and my) view is that successful procurement teams require multiple skills in procurement, negotiation, internal alignment, and the ability to build strategic plans—it's all about balance. Whether you have a four-person team or a sixty-five person team, you have to have these skills and you have to have the right mix of skills to ensure that you can both define strategic plans and meet the objectives of the strategic plan.

Strategic plans without internal organizational alignment will result in "ohms" or cultural non-intentional resistance. Strategic plans without individual deliverables clearly defined and skills assessed can result in individual frustration with inability to produce expected results (example, lacking core skills required) or missed expectations (higher skill set with misaligned deliverables). It's critically important to ensure individual and team dynamic skills are aligned with the strategic plan process and deliverables. If not, there is a great risk of increased management challenges with organizational trust and ability to drive to a common deliverable with a dynamic, leading-edge team.

The Procurement Effectiveness Continuum

A simple exercise is to evaluate your team based on a Procurement Effectiveness Continuum. For example, how is your procurement team perceived by the organization or different groups within the organization?

Support	Involved	Collaborative	Partner	Trusted Advisor	Advocate
Issue PO	Request Quote	Run RFP	Define Technology Roadmap	Leadership Team Member	CIO or Senior VP Endorsed

This exercise requires meeting with your stakeholders and understanding where your organization wants the procurement team to be, where the executive management team wants the procurement team to be and where you want procurement to be.

There is obviously huge value added by moving through the continuum; however, it is not a simple process and you have to own it. You have to obtain alignment from each major group in the organization. I used to say you need to earn a seat at the negotiation table, and once you get that seat, you have to ensure your team is equipped with the right skill-set to effectively prove their value and keep a seat at the table.

This ties into the whole tribal knowledge concept. You learn from each other to develop those skills and complete periodic assessments and course corrections to optimize skill development and growth.

Final Thoughts

I understand that the Win-Win-Win strategy is a radically different way of thinking from traditional procurement. That being said, it has been incredibly successful for me, over multiple companies, and over many negotiations with major tech corporations. It is my firm belief that this is the ultimate blueprint for a successful strategic procurement organization.

There are three things I want you to take away from this book. First, focus on stakeholder engagement, not savings targets. If you build the relationships with your stakeholders the spend and savings opportunities will come. Number two, the world requires collaboration more than ever today. Focus on the Win-Win-Win, versus just winning for your company. The third thing is more and more companies need the flexibility of the field of dreams mentality, so find suppliers that will go down that journey with you.

In short, I'd like you to reevaluate your current supplier/business relationship, look for suppliers that will be strategic partners of the future, develop Win-Win-Win strategies to invest in that relationship, and look to divest suppliers who won't join you in this journey.

If you want to learn more, or have questions for me, please feel free to reach out to me at win3procurement@gmail.com, I always welcome feedback (and the chance to grow my tribal knowledge).